Many parts of this puzzle are missing.
Can you still tell what it is?
If you think it's a picture of a dinosaur, you're right!
The parts that you could see helped you to decide what the missing parts must be.

What we know about dinosaurs is like this puzzle.
Many parts are missing.
There is much that we don't know.
But what we do know tells us many things about dinosaurs and how they lived.

Most dinosaurs were big, but there were little dinosaurs, too.

Some were more than 90 feet long.

Others were only two feet long.

No dinosaur was bigger than this one.

It was as heavy as 130 elephants.

It was bigger than a house.

Brachiosaurus

Some dinosaurs were so big
that they had to eat most of the time.
Most big dinosaurs ate plants,
but some ate meat.

These dinosaurs ate meat.
They had sharp teeth.

Tyrannosaurus

Most dinosaurs lived on land.

They moved around in different ways.

Most dinosaurs were not fast animals.

Very big dinosaurs took a long time
to get from place to place.

This dinosaur walked on all four feet.

Protocerotops

This dinosaur walked only
on its back feet.

Albertosaurus

Some dinosaurs lived part of the time in water and ate fish.

This dinosaur could swim in the water.

Cryptocleidus

Dinosaurs had to protect themselves from other dinosaurs.

They had different ways to protect themselves.

The horns on this dinosaur helped to protect it.

Triceratops

This dinosaur had very heavy scales
all over it.

These scales worked like armor
to protect the dinosaur.

The spikes on this dinosaur scared away hungry dinosaurs.

Ankylosaurus

This dinosaur had a long, long neck.

With its long neck, it could reach food that was high up in the trees.

It spent part of the time in water and part of the time on land.

It ate only plants.

Diplodocus

Most dinosaurs were slow, but some were fast.

This was the fastest dinosaur.

It would run away from danger.

It could run as fast as a car.

Struthiomimus

This animal was not a dinosaur, but it lived at the same time as dinosaurs.

It was the biggest flying animal that ever lived.

A group of these animals would attack dinosaurs.

They would attack even the biggest dinosaurs.

Pteranodon

Here is another animal that lived
in the time of the dinosaurs.
It lived in the water.

Tylosaurus

There are no dinosaurs living today.

If there were, we would know more
about the dinosaur puzzle.

Some people have found dinosaur bones
and eggs.

Some have found dinosaur footprints.

These bones, eggs, and footprints
are called fossils.

These are fossil bones from one of the bigger dinosaurs.

New parts of the dinosaur puzzle are found every day.

You can find out more about dinosaurs in the library.

The librarian can help you find a good dinosaur book.

One day, we may have all the parts of the dinosaur puzzle.